BEHOLD
THE LAMB OF GOD

60 Questions and Answers
on the Mystery of the Eucharist

EDWARD SRI

ASCENSION
West Chester, Pennsylvania

Ascension
PO Box 1990
West Chester, PA 19380
1-800-376-0520
ascensionpress.com

Cover design: Stella Ziegler

Printed in the United States of America
23 24 25 26 27 5 4 3 2 1

ISBN 978-1-954882-09-6 (paperback)
ISBN 978-1-954882-10-2 (e-book)

In memory of Fr. John Hardon, SJ,
whose devotion to and teaching on the Eucharist
have blessed countless souls.

CONTENTS

Preface

The Eucharist is not just one aspect of our Catholic Faith; it is the very center. As the US bishops explain, "*The Lord accompanies us in many ways, but none as profound as when we encounter him in the Eucharist.*"[1] Indeed, in the Eucharist, Jesus makes the loving sacrifice of his Body and Blood on the Cross present to us so that we can share in it, nourishes us with his very Body and Blood in Holy Communion, and remains close us in the Real Presence of the Blessed Sacrament.

Unfortunately, many Catholics today do not understand the profound gift the Eucharist is for their lives. Belief in the Real Presence of Christ in the Eucharist is declining, and Mass attendance in many areas is dropping. How do we proclaim this central mystery of our Faith in the world today?

This short booklet provides an easy-to-read overview of Catholic teaching on the Eucharist. It takes readers on a journey through the key aspects of Eucharistic theology and devotion. The question-and-answer format is intended to break things down in a simple way, addressing common questions, introducing foundational catechesis, and doing so in a concise, engaging, and inspiring manner, encouraging souls to go deeper in their love for Jesus in the Eucharist. This booklet can be used by families and individuals, distributed in parishes and adult faith formation programs, and used for RCIA and sacramental preparation.

INTRODUCTION TO THE EUCHARIST

1.   Why is the Eucharist so important?

Love wants to be near the one it loves. That is why the God who is love (see 1 John 4:8) chose to remain so intimately close to us and even unite himself to us in this most unique gift of his very Body and Blood in the Eucharist.

As you will discover in this book, the Eucharist is the most beautiful gift we have from God, for it is the gift of his very self. It is called the "source and summit of the Christian life"[2] because all we are and all we do as Christians flow from the Eucharist and lead us toward it. As the *Catechism of the Catholic Church* explains, the Eucharist is called the "Holy and Divine Liturgy" because all the Church's worship finds its most intense expression in the Eucharistic celebration (CCC 1330). It is called the "Holy Sacrifice" because it makes present Christ's loving sacrifice on the Cross and unites our lives with that love (CCC 1330). It is called the "medicine of immortality"[3] because in Holy Communion we receive healing from our sins and a foretaste of our heavenly home. It is also the "sacrament of love,"[4] as Jesus remains mysteriously present to us in the tabernacles in our churches, waiting for us to spend time with him in prayer and adoration.

2.   What is the Eucharist?

The Holy Eucharist is the supreme gift Jesus came to offer us—the gift of his very self and of his work of salvation. In short, the Eucharist is the sacred memorial of Christ's death and Resurrection. When the Eucharist is celebrated, that central event of our salvation truly becomes present, and our redemption is carried out. So important is this gift of himself that Jesus offered the sacrifice of his Body and Blood on the Cross and returned to the Father only after he left us the Eucharist as a way for us to really share in his sacrifice as if we had been present.

3.   When did Jesus institute the Eucharist?

Jesus instituted the Eucharist "on the night when he was betrayed" (1 Corinthians 11:23), the night of the day we know as Holy Thursday, while he was celebrating the Last Supper with his disciples. This meal took place in the context of the Jewish Feast of Passover.

4.   How did Jesus institute the Eucharist?

At the Last Supper, Jesus took bread, blessed and broke it, and gave it to his disciples, saying, "This is my Body, which will be given up for you." And after he took a chalice, he gave thanks and gave it to his disciples saying, "This is the chalice of my Blood, the Blood of the new and eternal covenant, which will be poured out for you and for many." And he told them, "Do this in memory of me."[5]

5.   What are the three main aspects of the Eucharist?

The Eucharist has three main aspects: the Eucharist as Holy Sacrifice, as Real Presence, and as Holy Communion.

- As *Holy Sacrifice*, the Eucharist makes present the sacrifice of Christ's Body and Blood on the Cross so that we can participate in it today and Christ's saving work may be applied to our lives. This is why the celebration of the Eucharist is traditionally called "The Holy Sacrifice of the Mass."

- As *Real Presence*, the Eucharist is the Body and Blood of Jesus under the appearance of bread and wine. The bread and wine at Mass are changed into the Body and Blood of Christ. The Eucharist, therefore, is not merely a symbol or a reminder of Jesus but the Real Presence of Jesus' Body and Blood.

- As *Holy Communion,* the Eucharist is Jesus' gift of himself to us. When we receive the Eucharist in Holy Communion, we receive Jesus and become one with him. We also are brought into deeper communion with our brothers and sisters in Christ in the Church.

THE EUCHARIST AS HOLY SACRIFICE

6. Why is the Eucharist called a sacrifice?

The Eucharist is called a sacrifice because it makes present the sacrifice of Christ on the Cross, the loving gift of himself that he offered for our salvation.

7. Is this just about *remembering* Jesus' sacrificial death?

No. It's so much more. The sacrificial gift of himself that Jesus offered on the Cross for our salvation some two thousand years ago is made present to us today at the celebration of the Eucharist. The Eucharist doesn't just recall Christ's death on the Cross. It actually makes that saving event present to us so that we can enter into it. When we go to Mass, we in a very real sense go to Calvary, for the mystery of the Cross is made present to us sacramentally. The sacrifice on the Cross and the Eucharistic sacrifice are the same sacrifice.

8. So is this about sacrificing Jesus over and over again?

No. It is the same sacrifice, but the manner of its offering is different. Jesus was sacrificed once and for all on the Cross. But that one, bloody sacrifice on Calvary is made present to us in the Eucharist in an unbloody way. As the *Catechism* explains, "In this divine sacrifice which is celebrated in the Mass, the same Christ who offered himself once in a bloody manner on the altar of the cross is contained and offered in an unbloody manner" (CCC 1367).

9. How can this be? Does Jesus ever teach about the Eucharist being a sacrifice?

Jesus instituted the Eucharist in the context of the great Jewish Feast of Passover, during which a lamb would be offered in sacrifice. At the Last Supper, he spoke about his Body and Blood in ways that would recall the sacrifice of the lambs for the Passover feast. He spoke of his Body being "given for" and his blood being "poured out" (Luke 22:19–20). In the first-century Jewish world, this language would have strong sacrificial overtones. It recalls the ancient Jewish sacrificial rites of the Temple, in which an animal's body was "offered up" and its blood was "poured out" in sacrifice.

By taking this sacrificial language from the Temple and applying it to his own Body and Blood, Jesus was already anticipating his sacrifice on the Cross. He was referring to his Body and Blood as being offered in sacrifice like that of a Passover Lamb.

10. **But where does Jesus say anything about the Eucharist *making present* his sacrifice on the Cross?**

Here we need to understand the Jewish background of Jesus' crucial words at the Last Supper, "Do this in memory of me."

For the ancient Jews, a memorial does not merely recall a past event. It makes that past event present. For example, when they celebrated the Passover, they did so as a liturgical memorial. That means they didn't just remember the foundational event in their people's history, when they were liberated from slavery in Egypt. They believed that when they celebrated the Passover each year, the original Passover event was mystically made present to them so they could participate in it. A biblical memorial makes the past event present.

Therefore, when Jesus said at the Last Supper, "Do this in memory of me," he was not telling the Apostles to perform a simple ritual meal that would help people remember him.

He was commanding the Apostles to celebrate the Last Supper as a liturgical memorial. Therefore, the heart of the Last Supper—the sacrificial offering of Christ's Body and Blood—would be made present to worshippers throughout the ages in the celebration of the Eucharist. As the *Catechism* explains, the Eucharist does not represent Christ's sacrifice on the cross merely symbolically; it "*re-presents* (makes present) the sacrifice of the cross" (CCC 1366, original emphasis). Indeed, the Body and Blood Jesus speaks of at the Last Supper are his Body and Blood sacrificed on Calvary, and this is what Jesus commanded the Apostles to make present in the celebration of the Eucharist.

11. Why is this sacrificial aspect of the Eucharist important for my life?

At any moment, the sacrifice of the Mass is absolutely the most amazing event happening in the world! Think about what's happening at every Liturgy: Through the Eucharistic sacrifice, the saving power of the Cross is unleashed in our lives in a unique way. As the sacrifice of Christ is made present ever anew at every Mass, Jesus is inviting us to be caught up into his perfect, self-giving love—his total gift of himself to the Father, his loving sacrifice.[6]

Jesus wants to live his sacrificial love ever more through us. He wants to transform us. He wants to heal our weak, selfish hearts and make our hearts more like his. And he does this in a most profound way, through our participation in the sacrifice of the Mass. The "bloody sacrifice which he was to accomplish once for all on the cross would be re-presented, its memory perpetuated until the end of the world, and its salutary power be applied to the forgiveness of the sins we daily commit."[7]

So if we want to grow in Christ-like, sacrificial love, the primary place this will happen is in the Mass, where we encounter Sacrificial Love himself most profoundly. And if we want the forgiveness of sins and the saving work of Christ to heal our souls, we will eagerly go to Mass, where the power of the Cross is applied to our lives most fully. This is why, of all the things happening in the world, the sacrifice of the Mass is by far the most amazing event in which we could ever participate!

12. What are some practical things I should do to participate more fully in the sacrifice of the Mass?

In the Mass, we have the opportunity to give ourselves to God in the most powerful way: we can unite our entire lives with Jesus' own loving gift of himself to the Father!

Therefore, we should join *all our prayers, works, joys, and sufferings* with Jesus' offering of himself. We can do this by not just going through the motions at Mass but reverently reciting the prayers throughout the Eucharistic Liturgy. We can see our lives symbolically being represented by the bread and wine presented to the priest at the offertory. When the priest says, "Pray, brethren, that my sacrifice and yours may be acceptable to God, the almighty Father," we can tell the Lord that we give him our entire lives in this Eucharistic sacrifice. Most of all, at the words of Consecration, we can tell Jesus in our hearts that we offer him our entire lives on the altar, praying that our sacrifice may be united with his perfect sacrificial gift of himself to the Father.

As the *Catechism* explains, "In the Eucharist the sacrifice of Christ becomes also the sacrifice of the members of his Body. The lives of the faithful, their praise, sufferings, prayer, and work, are united with those of Christ and with his total offering, and so acquire a new value. Christ's sacrifice present on the altar makes it possible for all generations of Christians to be united with his offering" (CCC 1368).

THE EUCHARIST AS REAL PRESENCE

13. Isn't the Eucharist just a symbol of Jesus?

No, the Eucharist is not merely a symbol of Jesus. Nor is Christ only spiritually present in some vague way in the bread and wine. At the Last Supper, Jesus took bread and wine and said, "This is my body. ... This is my blood." When the priest at Mass recites Jesus' words at the moment of Consecration, the bread and wine on the altar are changed into Christ's Body and Blood. They are no longer bread and wine. When we are in the presence of the Eucharist, we are in the midst of the Real Presence of Jesus Christ. Indeed, this is the supreme gift Jesus gives us: the gift of his very self, the Real Presence of his Body and Blood in the Eucharist!

14. But it still looks and tastes like bread and wine?

This change of the bread and wine into the Body and Blood of Christ is not a chemical one. All the outward, sensible appearances of bread and wine remain. The Host still looks like bread, tastes like bread, and feels like bread. And the chalice contains what to all the senses appears to be ordinary wine. The chemical structures of bread and wine remain the same. But underneath these appearances, Jesus' Body and Blood are really present in the Eucharist.

The theological term used to describe this change is *transubstantiation*, which expresses how, by the Consecration of the bread and wine, "there takes place a change of the whole substance of the bread into the substance of the body of Christ our Lord and of the whole substance of the wine into the substance of his blood"[8] (CCC 1376). Put simply, the substance, the very reality of the bread and wine, is changed into the Body and Blood of Christ. Even though the outward characteristics of bread and wine (the "Eucharistic species") remain the same, we

encounter Jesus himself, his very Body and Blood, Soul and
Divinity, made present under sacramental signs, whenever
we encounter the Eucharist.

15. **Where in the Bible does Jesus say he is going to give
us his Real Presence in the Eucharist?**

When Jesus himself taught about the Eucharist, he used
language with a profound realism to describe how we will
partake of his Body and Blood. Not only did Jesus say at
the Last Supper "This is my body. ... This is my blood,"
but earlier, when he gave his most extensive teaching
on the Eucharist, he said we must really *eat* his flesh and
drink his blood. So important was the partaking of his
actual Body and Blood in the Eucharist that he said the
following words in what is known as his Bread of Life
discourse: "I am the living bread which came down from
heaven; if any one eats of this bread, he will live for ever;
and the bread which I shall give for the life of the world
is my flesh" (John 6:51).

16. **Did the original hearers think Jesus was really
claiming to give us his Body and Blood to eat
and drink?**

Yes. In the Bread of Life discourse, Jesus says, "I am the
bread of life" (John 6:35), and makes it clear that he is not
speaking in a vague, figurative way: "The bread which I
shall give for the life of the world *is my flesh*" (John 6:51,
emphasis added).

The people listening were shocked at this. They said, "How
can this man give us his flesh to eat?" (John 6:52). Notice
that they didn't think Jesus was speaking metaphorically.
They understood Jesus very well. They knew that he was

speaking realistically here, and that's why they were horrified and couldn't accept what he was saying.

17. **But could Jesus have been speaking figuratively here, just using a metaphor, when he spoke about eating his flesh and drinking his blood?**

Jesus easily could have clarified his teaching if he sensed that people were misunderstanding him. In other words, if Jesus had been teaching in a figurative way, he could have said, "Hold on. You misunderstood me. I was just speaking metaphorically here!" He could have clarified his teaching, saying, "Let me explain. You don't *really* need to eat my flesh. You just need to feed yourself with my wisdom and my love."

But that is exactly what Jesus did *not* do. In fact, he got even more explicit. When the people listening objected to the idea of eating his flesh, Jesus responded by using even more graphic, intense language to put his meaning beyond the shadow of a doubt, making it perfectly clear that we really do need to partake of his flesh and his blood: "Truly, truly, I say to you, unless you eat the flesh of the Son of man and drink his blood, you have no life in you; he who eats my flesh and drinks my blood has eternal life, and I will raise him up at the last day. For my flesh is food indeed, and my blood is drink indeed. He who eats my flesh and drinks my blood abides in me, and I in him" (John 6:53–56).

Jesus would not have spoken like this if he were only using a metaphor. He clearly wants to give us his very Body and Blood in the Eucharist. In fact, he now uses a word for "eat" that has even greater graphic intensity—*trogein*, which means "to chew or gnaw"—not a word that would be used figuratively here!

18. **In the end, how did the people respond to Jesus'**
    teaching on the Eucharist?

    This teaching was too difficult for some people to accept.
    The crowds were aghast. Even many of Jesus' disciples
    rejected him over this teaching and left him (John 6:66).

    But what is crucial is that *Jesus let them go*. He didn't
    chase after them, saying, "Wait! You misunderstood me!"
    They understood quite well that Jesus was talking about
    really partaking of his flesh and blood, and they rejected
    his teaching. So important is the gift of himself in the
    Eucharist that Jesus let his disciples walk away if they could
    not accept this supreme gift. He wants to be so intimately
    close to us in the Eucharist that he makes the partaking of
    his Body and Blood a crucial test for being a true disciple.

19. **Isn't God present everywhere? How is the**
    Eucharist different?

    God is present to his people in many ways. In the
    most foundational way, God is omnipresent—present
    everywhere—by virtue of his power in holding everything
    in existence. The stars, this book in your hand, even your
    very life would cease to exist if God did not keep it in
    existence moment by moment by his power.

    But God is even closer to us in profound spiritual ways.
    Christ is present in a special way in the poor, in his Word,
    in the sacraments, and in the prayer of two or more who
    gather in his name.

    Even more, however, Jesus is uniquely present in the
    Eucharist. For the Eucharist is the very Body and Blood,
    Soul and Divinity of Jesus Christ. Through the Eucharist,
    "Christ, God and man, makes himself wholly and entirely
    present."[9] Therefore, when we encounter the Eucharist,
    we encounter the same Jesus who walked the streets of

Galilee two thousand years ago, made present to us now
under the sacramental signs of bread and wine.

20. So when I receive the Eucharist, am I really eating Jesus? Is this cannibalism?

Cannibals eat dead human flesh. What we receive in Holy
Communion, in contrast, is fully alive. It is the glorified
Body of the Risen Christ. Jesus' resurrected Body is a
completely transformed "spiritual body" (1 Corinthians
15:44). It is different from our ordinary human bodies,
which are confined by time and space. The Body of the
resurrected Jesus, for example, could pass through walls,
appear in different ways, suddenly appear, and suddenly
disappear. In the Eucharist, the Risen Body of Christ is
present sacramentally under the appearance of bread
and wine.

21. When are the bread and wine changed into Christ's Body and Blood?

The *Catechism* explains that the Eucharistic presence
of Christ "begins at the moment of the consecration"
(CCC 1377). "In the institution narrative, the power of
the words and the action of Christ, and the power of the
Holy Spirit, make sacramentally present under the species
of bread and wine Christ's body and blood, his sacrifice
offered on the cross once for all" (CCC 1353).

22. Is the Blood of Christ present only in the chalice? And is the Body of Christ present only in the consecrated Host?

No. The whole of Christ—Body and Blood, Soul and
Divinity—is sacramentally present under each of the
species, the outward appearances of bread and wine. If

someone receives only the sacred Host, he receives the Body *and* Blood of Christ. Similarly, if someone cannot receive the sacred Host (because of celiac disease, for example), he or she still receives the Body and Blood of Christ when drinking from the chalice at Mass.

Receiving the Host alone has been the most common form of reception in the Latin Rite. But the *Catechism* explains that "the sign of communion is more complete when given under both kinds, since in that form the sign of the Eucharistic meal appears more clearly."[10]

THE EUCHARIST as HOLY COMMUNION

23. Why is receiving Holy Communion so important?

The whole Eucharistic sacrifice is directed toward union with Christ in Holy Communion. When we receive the Eucharist, we are receiving Christ himself! Feel the weight of that profound reality: in those moments after receiving Communion, God is dwelling within us in the most intimate union we can have with him on earth. God not only comes upon our altars, under the appearance of bread and wine at every Mass—that alone would be amazing! He also enters our bodies, desiring to join himself to our souls in every Holy Communion. As Pope Francis teaches, "The Eucharist is essential for us: it is Christ who wishes to enter our lives and fill us with his grace."[11]

24. Why does Jesus give himself as food and drink?

He does so because he loves us and wants to be united to us. In Scripture, the body expresses the whole person. And the blood is seen as containing life. So when Jesus gives us his Body and Blood to consume, he is expressing his desire to give his entire self to us and to fill us with his life.

25. Where does the Bible teach about the importance of receiving Holy Communion?

At the Last Supper, Jesus commanded the Apostles to eat his Body and drink his Blood. In the Bread of Life discourse, he emphasized the importance of this: "Unless you eat the flesh of the Son of man and drink his blood you have no life in you" (John 6:53). St. Paul also affirms the importance of partaking of the one bread of the Eucharist: "The cup of blessing which we bless, is it not a participation in the blood of Christ? The bread which we break, is it not a participation in the body of Christ?" (1 Corinthians 10:16).

26. **But if Jesus already offered his sacrifice on the Cross for our sins, why do we still need Holy Communion?**

In Scripture, the communion meal was the climax of the ritual sacrifice. It was not enough, for example, to sacrifice a lamb for Passover. You had to *eat* the lamb. The eating of the lamb that had been offered to God was a symbolic action sealing union between God and the person offering the sacrifice. If, however, an Israelite in Egypt sacrificed the Passover lamb but didn't eat the lamb, he would not have completed the Passover and he would not have forged his covenant with God.

This threefold Biblical pattern of a *sacrifice* followed by a *communion meal* that forges *covenant union* is what St. Paul assumes when he shows the connection between Christ's sacrifice on the Cross and the festive communion meal of the Eucharist: "For our paschal lamb, Christ, has been *sacrificed.* Therefore let us celebrate *the feast*" (1 Corinthians 5:7–8 NAB, emphasis added). Paul makes clear that this feast of Christ's sacrifice is the communion meal of the Eucharist (see 1 Corinthians 10–11).

27. **What are the fruits of receiving Holy Communion?**

Holy Communion is our most important spiritual food, and it bears much fruit in our spiritual lives: it deepens our union with God, brings forgiveness of venial sins, helps preserve us from future mortal sins, makes us more committed to the poor, and strengthens our fellowship with others in the Body of Christ, the Church. It is a pledge of the glory to come, a foretaste of heaven where we will be at one with God for eternity. Pope Francis explains that "the Eucharist heals because it unites with Jesus: it makes us assimilate his way of living, his ability to break himself apart and give himself to brothers and sisters, to respond to evil with good."[12]

28. How should I prepare for a worthy reception of Holy Communion?

We should prepare for this union with Christ by observing the one-hour fast before receiving Communion. When we attend Mass, we also should have a spirit of prayer and recollection and a bodily demeanor in our gestures and in our dress that shows respect for the most noble guest whom we are about to welcome into our souls. Going to Reconciliation frequently is important (and for confessing mortal sins, essential) for a worthy reception of our Lord in the Eucharist.

29. How often should I receive?

If we have the proper dispositions, we are encouraged to receive every time we participate in the Mass. At minimum, we should receive once a year during the Easter season. But it is recommended that we receive every Sunday, on feast days, and if possible, even daily. A lay person who has already received Communion may receive it again on the same day but only within a Mass in which he or she is participating.[13]

30. What should I do after I receive?

Taking time for prayer and thanksgiving after receiving Holy Communion is so important. We should want to rest with our Lord dwelling within in us in these most intimate moments after Holy Communion. We should thank him for his many blessings, especially the gift of himself in the Eucharist. We should pour out our hearts to him, praising him, telling him we love him, presenting our needs to him, and interceding for others. We should take time quietly to listen to Jesus.

When we come back to our pews after receiving Holy Communion, this is not the time to look around and see who's at Mass. This is not the time to develop your parking lot exit strategy or ponder the coffee and donuts. This is a time to rest with our Beloved Jesus. This is why the tradition of taking time for prayer and thanksgiving after Communion is so important. Even after Mass is finished, we don't need to rush out the door. We can spend a few minutes with our Lord in prayer. If we don't take time to talk to Jesus and listen to him while he's dwelling within us after Holy Communion, when will we ever really take time to do this?

31. For how long does Jesus' Real Presence remain inside me after Holy Communion?

The *Catechism* teaches that Christ's presence "endures as long as the Eucharistic species subsist" (CCC 1377). Though no specific amount of time is given by the *Catechism*, some suggest that the Eucharistic species (the outward appearance of bread and wine) endure in our bodies for about fifteen minutes.

32. What are the requirements for receiving Holy Communion?

One must be fully incorporated into the Catholic Church and be in the state of grace—not conscious of being in mortal sin. Anyone conscious of having committed a mortal sin must receive absolution in the Sacrament of Reconciliation before receiving Holy Communion. St. Paul warns us that "whoever, therefore, eats the bread or drinks the cup of the Lord in an unworthy manner will be guilty of profaning the body and blood of the Lord. Let a man examine himself, and so eat of the bread and drink of the cup. For any one who eats and drinks without discerning the body eats and drinks judgment upon himself" (1 Corinthians 11:27–29).

33. Why can't non-Catholics receive Holy Communion?

The Eucharist is the very Body and Blood of Christ. Non-Catholics who do not believe in the Real Presence of Jesus in the Eucharist would not be prepared to worthily receive Holy Communion. They could not sincerely say "Amen" ("I believe") when the priest says "The Body of Christ."

Moreover, the Eucharist is not just about communion with Christ; it is also a profound expression of communion with others who are united in the Catholic Church. For Holy Communion is a sign of unity in belief, worship, and life within the Church that non-Catholics do not yet share. Even if some non-Catholics were to say they believed in the Eucharist, we must realize that the "Amen" we say to "The Body of Christ" is not just affirming the truth of the Real Presence. It's also an acceptance of the teachings of the Church and an expression of unity—of communion— with the Church.

34. Do other non-Catholic churches have the Eucharist?

Some do, and some do not.

First, let's consider the Eastern Churches that are not in full communion with the Catholic Church (for example, the Orthodox Churches). Though they are separated from the Catholic Church, they still have apostolic succession— the handing on of authority from the Apostles to their successors (the bishops) throughout the centuries by the laying on of hands. Therefore, these Churches do possess real sacraments, the priesthood, and the Eucharist, which still joins them to us.[14]

Second, the ecclesial communities that are rooted in the Protestant Reformation are separated from the Catholic Church, and they "have not preserved the proper reality of the Eucharistic mystery in its fullness, especially because of the absence of the sacrament of Holy Orders."[15] Without proper apostolic succession (which is necessary for the valid ordination of bishops and priests), these communities are unable to celebrate the Eucharist. Nevertheless, "when they commemorate the Lord's death and resurrection in the Holy Supper," they "profess that it signifies life in communion with Christ and await his coming in glory."[16]

35. Can I receive communion in these other non-Catholic churches?

Because the Eastern Churches, through apostolic succession, still have the priesthood, the sacraments, and the Eucharist, communion is possible and even encouraged "given suitable circumstances and the approval of Church authority."[17]

But since the ecclesial communities rooted in the Reformation have not maintained the Sacrament of Holy Orders and the full reality of the Eucharistic mystery, "Eucharistic intercommunion with these communities is not possible" (CCC 1400). The sad realities of division within Christ's Body urge us all to pray that the full unity of all Christian believers may one day be restored (see CCC 1398).

36. Are there any circumstances in which Holy Communion may be given to other Christians?

Catholic ministers may give Holy Communion to members of those Eastern churches that are not in full communion with the Catholic Church but possess the sacraments, the priesthood, and apostolic succession, if they ask for it of their own accord and have the required disposition. Members of other ecclesial communities (those derived from the Protestant Reformation) may be given Holy Communion only in grave situations, if they ask for it, have the required disposition, and exhibit evidence of believing what the Church teaches about the Eucharist.[18]

37. What do I do at Mass if I cannot receive Holy Communion?

We might not be in a state to receive Communion for various reasons—for example, not being in a state of grace, not being Catholic, or not having observed the one-hour fast before Communion.

In those circumstances, we still can make a spiritual communion, a prayer expressing our desire to receive Jesus in Holy Communion. Here is a traditional Act of Spiritual Communion that was written by St. Alphonsus Liguori:

> My Jesus, I believe that you are truly present in the Most Holy Sacrament.
> I love you above all things, and I desire to possess you within my soul.
> Since I cannot now receive you sacramentally, come at least spiritually into my heart.
> I embrace you as being already there and unite myself wholly to you.
> Never permit me to be separated from you. Amen.

Also, some priests might invite people who cannot receive Holy Communion to come forward in the communion line to receive a blessing.

38. **I've seen some people receive Communion on the tongue and some receive in the hand. What does the Church say about this?**

    The faithful in the United States may receive the Eucharist on the tongue or in the hand.

    The Church teaches that the faithful have the right to receive Holy Communion on the tongue. But if a communicant, by his choice, desires to receive in the hand, Holy Communion may be administered in the hand where the bishops' conference has given permission. In the dioceses in the United States, the bishops allow this.[19]

39. **How could I ever be worthy to receive Holy Communion?**

    It is fitting that just prior to receiving Holy Communion, we pray, "Lord, *I am not worthy* that you should enter under my roof, but only say the word and my soul shall be healed" (emphasis added). This prayer, inspired by the humility of the Roman centurion (see Matthew 8:5–13), teaches us two important lessons. The first is that we should approach the Eucharist with great humility and reverence. On our own, we are not worthy to receive this amazing gift of the Real Presence of Christ into our souls. The second is that this is a gift God desires to give us. God *wants* us to receive him in the Eucharist, and he can help us worthily receive him through the sacramental graces of Baptism and Reconciliation. In fact, the Eucharist itself cleanses us of venial sins, so we should not be afraid to approach Christ in Holy Communion if we have properly prepared ourselves to do so.

40. If I choose to receive in the hand, is there a particular way I should do that?

First, the Church teaches that "special care should be taken to ensure that the host is consumed by the communicant in the presence of the minister, so that no one goes away carrying the Eucharistic species in his hand. If there is a risk of profanation, then Holy Communion should not be given in the hand to the faithful."[20]

Moreover, the USCCB explains, "If Communion is received in the hand, the hands should first of all be clean. If one is right-handed, the left hand should rest upon the right. The host will then be laid in the palm of the left hand and then taken by the right hand to the mouth. If one is left-handed this is reversed. It is not appropriate to reach out with the fingers and take the host from the person distributing."[21]

Finally, catechesis on the Real Presence of Jesus in the Eucharist and on reverential care for the sacred Host in the throne of one's hand is paramount, since even particles of the consecrated Host are the Body and Blood of Christ: "On the part of both the minister and the recipient, whenever the host is placed in the hand of a communicant there must be careful concern and caution, especially about particles that might fall from the hosts. The usage of communion in the hand must be accompanied by relevant instruction or catechesis on Catholic teaching regarding Christ's real and permanent presence under the eucharistic elements and the proper reverence toward this sacrament."[22]

41. **What does the Church say about receiving Holy Communion standing or kneeling?**

The Church allows the faithful to receive Holy Communion standing or kneeling, according to the norms established by the local bishops' conference. In the United States, the norm is that "Holy Communion is to be received standing, unless an individual member of the faithful wishes to receive Communion while kneeling." A bow is the act of reverence made by those receiving.[23]

THE EUCHARIST IN THE MASS

42. Why is the celebration of the Eucharist called "the Mass"?

This tradition of calling the Eucharistic celebration "the Mass" comes from the closing prayer of the Liturgy and makes an important point.

In the ancient world, assemblies typically closed with a formal dismissal. The early Christians incorporated a similar conclusion to their Eucharistic liturgies. From the fourth century, the Latin words *Ite missa est* were employed for this purpose. Literally meaning "Go, you are dismissed," these words are rendered in the translation of the Mass as "Go forth, the Mass is ended."

It is significant that the whole Liturgy receives its name from the Latin word *missa* ("dismissal" or "sending") in its closing line. This points to how the Mass ultimately is a sending forth. As the *Catechism* explains, the celebration of the Eucharist is called Holy Mass (*Missa*) "because the liturgy in which the mystery of salvation is accomplished concludes with the sending forth (*missio*) of the faithful, so that they may fulfill God's will in their daily lives" (CCC 1332). The closing prayer of the Liturgy, therefore, is not an aimless dismissal. It is a dismissal with a mission. It is a sending forth of God's people to bring the mysteries of Christ's Passion, death, and Resurrection into the world.

43. When did Christians begin celebrating the Mass?

The Church began celebrating the Eucharist from the very beginning of Christianity, obedient to Jesus' command at the Last Supper: "Do this in memory of me." The earliest disciples after Pentecost dedicated themselves to "the breaking of the bread," a reference to the Eucharistic celebration (Acts 2:42). St. Paul describes the celebration of Eucharist in his letter to the Corinthians (see 1 Corinthians

10:16–21; 11:17–34). The *Didache*, a Christian manual
from around the start of the second century, described
how Christians gathered on Sunday to break bread and
give thanks and celebrate the sacrifice of the Lord. St.
Ignatius of Antioch exhorted Christians to participate in
only the one Eucharist, the one celebrated by the bishop
or someone he appoints.[24] Even a Roman governor, Pliny
the Younger, in AD 112 reported Christians assembling
before sunrise for this sacred meal.[25]

44. What did those early celebrations look like?

Already around the year AD 155, St. Justin Martyr described
the basic outline of the Mass we have today.[26] Christians
gathered together on Sunday and read from the writings
of the prophets and Apostles (Old and New Testament
readings). The presider gave an exhortation to live out
the Christian Faith (a homily) and rose to offer prayers of
petition to God (Prayer of the Faithful). Bread and a cup of
wine and water were given to the presider (Presentation
of the Gifts) who offered them to God and gave thanks
(*eucharistein* in Greek) (the Eucharistic Prayer), and at
the conclusion of the prayer of thanksgiving, the people
said together, "Amen" (the Great Amen). Deacons gave
the people the "eucharisted" bread and wine (Holy
Communion) and took them to those who were absent.

Many of the prayers we recite in the Mass today have roots
in the first few centuries of Christianity. St. Hippolytus
of Rome, for example, writing about AD 215, seems to
preserve prayers and rituals from the Eucharistic Liturgy
of the second century. Here we find the fundamental
structure of the Eucharistic prayers we hear today:
prayers of thanksgiving, the words of institution, the
commemoration and offering, invocation of the Holy

Spirit, the doxology, and the Amen. Consider the following prayers, which are almost exactly the same as what we recite today:

> The bishop says: The Lord be with you.
> And all reply: And with your spirit.
> The bishop says: Lift up your hearts.
> The people respond: We have them with the Lord.
> The bishop says: Let us give thanks to the Lord.
> The people respond: It is proper and just.[27]

Indeed, when we participate in the Mass, we enter a tradition of rituals and prayers that go back to the first centuries of Christianity!

45. How often must we go to Mass?

We must participate in Mass every Sunday and on Holy Days of Obligation (which are special celebrations of the saving work God has accomplished for us through Christ and his saints). But many people also go to Mass occasionally during the week. Some people go to Mass every day.

46. But why do we *have* to go to Mass?

We owe God worship. As a prayer at Mass states, "It is truly right and just, our duty and our salvation, always and everywhere to give you thanks." And we must worship God the way he desires. This is a crucial point: When it comes to our worship of God, what's most important is not our personal preferences but what God himself has revealed about how we are to worship him. And as we've seen, Jesus commanded the Apostles to celebrate the Eucharist as the central act of worship. As the US bishops have explained, "To worship God on Sundays, then, is not the mere observance of a rule but the fulfillment of our identity, of who we are as members of the Body of Christ. Participation in the Mass is an act of love."[28]

47. But why can't I just worship God on my own?

As Christians, we should pray and worship God throughout our lives. But when we come to Mass, we enter the most perfect act of love, prayer, and worship. For Christ's sacrifice on the Cross, his total gift of himself to the Father, is the perfect act of worship. And as we've seen, that sacrifice of his Body and Blood is made present at the Mass so that we can join our lives with that perfect act of worship and be transformed by it. It is this central act of Eucharistic worship that Christians have been celebrating for two thousand years, ever since Jesus commanded the Apostles to offer the Lord's Supper.

48. Who can celebrate the Mass?

Only a validly ordained priest or bishop can celebrate the Eucharist and consecrate the bread and wine at Mass.

49. Why does it have to be a priest?

As Pope Francis once said, "The Eucharist isn't a reunion of friends who come to pray and eat bread and wine. The Eucharist is fundamentally priestly."[29] At the Last Supper, Jesus commanded the Apostles to celebrate the Eucharist: "Do this in memory of me." It was then that they were ordained as priests, given power to offer the sacrifice of the Lord's Supper and confect the Eucharist.

That priestly office has been handed down from the Apostles to their successors, the bishops, throughout the ages through the laying on of hands in the Sacrament of

Holy Orders. The bishops share their consecration and mission with the priests who, through the Sacrament of Holy Orders, become coworkers with their bishop in the mission Christ entrusted to the Apostles. It is in the celebration of the Eucharist that they exercise their priestly office most fully, acting in the person of Christ (*in persona Christi*), offering the sacrifice of the Mass, and confecting the Eucharist, changing the bread and wine into the Body and Blood of Christ.

50. What should I do to prepare for Mass?

It's important not just to walk into Mass as if you were attending an ordinary event, but to prepare your heart and mind to encounter God himself in the sacred Liturgy. We need to transition from our normal routines in the world to the sacredness of the Mass. One way to prepare for Mass is to take time beforehand to prayerfully review the readings from the Liturgy of the Word. We can do this at home or at church. We can also arrive at church early so that we have some time to quiet ourselves and pray before Mass begins. This is not the time to be talking to people around us. We want to prepare our hearts to encounter God. At a minimum, we are required to fast one hour before we receive Holy Communion and to enter into a spirit of prayer and recollection.

EUCHARISTIC DEVOTION OUTSIDE OF MASS

51. Does Christ's Presence in the Eucharist remain with us even outside of Mass?

Christ wanted to stay close to us in a unique way. Before he gave his life for our sins, he gave us the gift of his Real Presence in the Eucharist. That Real Presence of Christ remains with us in the consecrated Hosts that are kept in the tabernacle even outside of Mass. As St. Teresa of Calcutta (Mother Teresa) reportedly once said, "When you look at the crucifix, you understand how much Jesus loved you then. When you look at the Sacred Host, you understand how much Jesus loves you now."[30]

52. What is the tabernacle?

The tabernacle is a liturgical fixture that houses the Eucharist outside of Mass. It is box or cabinet typically made of gold that should be constructed in a way and given a worthy place that highlights the Real Presence of Christ in the Eucharist (see CCC 1379).

The word *tabernacle* means "dwelling place" and was used in Scripture to describe the "tent of meeting" that housed the cloud of God's glory, the visible manifestation of God's holy presence in ancient Israel. It is a fitting word to describe the sacred vessels in our churches that house the Real Presence—the Body and Blood, Soul and Divinity—of Jesus in the Eucharist. A candle is lit all day near the tabernacle as a reminder of Christ's presence with us.

53. What is the purpose of the tabernacle?

The tabernacle was originally intended as a dignified place to reserve the sacred Hosts that were to be brought to the sick and dying outside of Mass. It became a place for the faithful to pray and adore Christ present in the Eucharist.

It is a safe place to store consecrated Hosts, protecting them from being desecrated. The law of the Church states that the tabernacle is to be "immovable, made of solid and opaque material, and locked so that the danger of profanation may be entirely avoided."[31]

54. How should we show reverence to Jesus and worship him in the Eucharist?

We show our faith in the Eucharist not only during the Liturgy but also outside of Mass by giving the Sacrament of the Eucharist the worship that is due to God alone, for Christ's Real Presence remains in the consecrated Hosts. We express this worship in many ways: by bowing deeply or genuflecting (kneeling) before the tabernacle which houses Christ's Real Presence under the species of bread and wine, by reserving the consecrated Hosts with the greatest care and reverence, by exposing the sacred Hosts for the faithful to venerate in Eucharistic Adoration, and by bearing the sacred Hosts in solemn Eucharistic processions.[32]

55. What is the difference between Adoration and Exposition of the Blessed Sacrament?

Eucharistic *Adoration* refers to the worship of our Lord in the Blessed Sacrament. We express our adoration in many ways: genuflecting toward the tabernacle that contains the Blessed Sacrament, kneeling before the tabernacle, and sitting in silent prayer before Christ's Real Presence in the Eucharist. The Church encourages us to make frequent visits to adore the Blessed Sacrament kept in the tabernacle.[33]

Exposition of the Blessed Sacrament is a more focused form of Eucharistic Adoration that is part of the Church's liturgical life. It is a solemn rite in which the sacred Host is displayed for public worship. This can take place in a simple way by opening the tabernacle doors or in its fullest form when the consecrated Host is placed in a sacred vessel called a *monstrance* (based on the Latin word *monstrare*, which means "to show"), so that it can be easily seen and adored.

56. What is Benediction?

Benediction of the Blessed Sacrament is a rite in which the priest leads the faithful through a series of traditional prayers and hymns of Eucharistic Adoration and blesses the people with the sacred Host.

57. What is Perpetual Adoration?

Some religious communities and parishes offer Perpetual Exposition, when the Blessed Sacrament is exposed for worship for long periods of time, often throughout every day and night. Members of the community or parish take turns to pray before Jesus in the Blessed Sacrament, often for an hour or more at a time.

58. How do these Eucharistic devotions bring me closer to God?

Simply drawing near to Christ's loving presence in the Eucharist is a tremendous blessing for our spiritual lives. As Blessed Carlo Acutis once said, when "we face the sun, we become tan ... but when we place ourselves in front of the Eucharistic Jesus, we become saints."[34]

The same Jesus who walked the streets of Galilee two thousand years ago—the same Jesus who performed miracles, healed the sick, comforted the suffering, strengthened the weak, and calmed the storms—continues to be present to us sacramentally today in the Blessed Sacrament. In the Gospels, people drew near to Jesus to seek his guidance, his help, and his comfort. They also drew near because they loved him and wanted to follow him. And we can do the same.

Indeed, that same Jesus is longing for you to draw near to him in the Blessed Sacrament. He wants to be very close to you. He is present in all the tabernacles in churches and chapels throughout the world. He wants you to come to him with whatever is troubling you. He wants you to rest in his presence. He longs for your heart to make time for him. As St. John Paul II once said, "Jesus awaits us in this sacrament of love. Let us not refuse the time to go to meet him in adoration, in contemplation full of faith, and open to making amends for the serious offenses and crimes of the world. Let our adoration never cease."[35]

59. How does the Eucharist lead me closer to the poor?

The Church emphasizes the connection between Eucharistic devotion and care for the poor. As Pope Francis explains, "The one who is fed and nourished by the very body and blood of Christ cannot remain unaffected when he sees his brothers suffering want and hunger."[36] Take, for example, the witness of Mother Teresa. By recognizing Jesus' presence in the Eucharist under the appearance of bread and wine, she also was able to see the face of Christ in those who are poor and suffering. "We must pray to Jesus to give us that tenderness of the Eucharist. Unless we believe and see Jesus in the appearance of bread on the altar, we will not be able to see him in the distressing disguise of the poor."[37]

St. John Chrysostom warned against a Eucharistic devotion that neglects the poor: "Do you wish to honor the body of Christ? Do not ignore him when he is naked. Do not pay homage in the temple clad in silk only then to neglect him outside where he suffers cold and nakedness. He who said: 'This is my body' is the same One who said: 'You saw me hungry and you gave me no food.'"[38]

60. How can I grow in Eucharistic devotion? Practically, what can I do?

First, simply tell Jesus that you want to spend more time with him in Eucharistic devotion. Ask him to help you do so.

Second, *find a time* in your schedule when you can stop by a parish to visit Jesus in the Blessed Sacrament. It can be praying before the tabernacle in a church or in an Adoration chapel that has Perpetual Exposition of the Blessed Sacrament. Maybe you can make a quick visit for just a few minutes on your way to work or in between errands during the day. Maybe you can spend a longer period of time, such as a Holy Hour, once a week in his Eucharistic presence. Or perhaps you could go to a weekday Mass. Some Catholics even try to go to Mass every day.

Third, whenever you enter a church or chapel and are in the presence of the tabernacle containing the sacred Hosts, remember that you are entering holy ground. You are coming before Christ's Eucharistic Presence. God is there in the Blessed Sacrament. So take at least a moment to kneel in humble and reverent adoration before the Blessed Sacrament in the tabernacle (or before the monstrance if there is Exposition of the Eucharist). If you are only there for a few minutes, say a short prayer. You can simply tell Jesus you love him and that you are just stopping by to say a quick hello. If you have more time, you can incorporate the various kinds of prayer, including *adoration* (praising and worshipping Jesus for who he is as God), *thanksgiving* (expressing gratitude for his many blessings), *contrition* (telling Jesus you are sorry for your sins), *intercession* (prayers for other people), and *petition* (prayers for your own needs). You can also spend time in prayerful meditation on Scripture or another spiritual book. Or you can simply sit quietly in his holy Presence.

PRAYERS FOR EUCHARISTIC DEVOTION

Anima Christi

Soul of Christ, sanctify me.
Body of Christ, save me.
Blood of Christ, inebriate me.
Water from the side of Christ, wash me.
Passion of Christ, strengthen me.

O good Jesus, hear me.
Within Thy wounds hide me.
Never let me be separated from Thee.
From the malignant enemy, defend me.
At the hour of death, call me
and close to Thee bid me
that with Thy saints I may praise Thee forever and
    ever. Amen.

The Divine Praises

Blessed be God.
Blessed be his Holy Name.
Blessed be Jesus Christ, true God and true Man.
Blessed be the Name of Jesus.
Blessed be his Most Sacred Heart.
Blessed be his Most Precious Blood.
Blessed be Jesus in the Most Holy Sacrament of the Altar.
Blessed be the Holy Spirit, the Paraclete.
Blessed be the great Mother of God, Mary Most Holy.
Blessed be her Holy and Immaculate Conception.
Blessed be her Glorious Assumption.
Blessed be the name of Mary, Virgin and Mother.
Blessed be St. Joseph, her most chaste spouse.
Blessed be God in his angels and in his saints. Amen.

Prayer of Faith in the Eucharist

My good Jesus,
I believe with a firm and lively faith
that in this adorable sacrament are your Body and Blood,
Soul and Divinity.
I believe that in this consecrated Host
I shall receive that same Body
which was born of the most pure Virgin Mary in Bethlehem,
which suffered so many pains and torments for love of me
on the Way of the Cross and on Calvary,
and which rose gloriously the third day from the dead.
I believe that I shall receive God himself.

I adore you, O my God, as my Creator,
my Preserver, my Redeemer, and my Judge,
truly present in the Holy Eucharist.
Divine Host, I adore you
with the angels who fill the sanctuary
and hover over the tabernacle
as they hovered over the cave of Bethlehem in the holy night.
I adore you, my God,
with the Blessed Virgin
and in union with all the saints.
Lord and Master of the universe,
who has fixed your dwelling among men,
I adore you with profound gratitude.

O my Jesus, bless this temple where you reside
but still more the heart that I offer you
as a living abode and place of rest.
Deign ever to inhabit it by your grace and your love,
and may my sins never banish you from it!

Lord, I have a firm faith,
but do strengthen my faith
and animate it so that it may produce in my soul

deeper sentiments of adoration and love.
Good Lord, increase my faith that I may love you more
and be more generous in my sacrifices
for love of you and for the love of my neighbors. Amen. [39]

Short Prayer after Communion

Sweet Jesus,
Body and Blood most holy,
be the delight and pleasure of my soul,
my strength and salvation in all temptations,
my joy and peace in every trial,
my light and guide in every word and deed,
and my final protection in death. Amen.

– St. Thomas Aquinas

An Act of Spiritual Communion

My Jesus, I believe that you are truly present in the Most
   Holy Sacrament.
I love you above all things, and I desire to possess you within
   my soul.
Since I cannot now receive you sacramentally,
come at least spiritually into my heart.
I embrace you as being already there
and unite myself wholly to you.
Never permit me to be separated from you.

– St. Alphonsus Liguori

Prayer of Thanksgiving After Mass

Lord, Father all-powerful and ever-living God, I thank you,
for even though I am a sinner, your unprofitable servant, not
because of my worth but in the kindness of your mercy, you
have fed me with the Precious Body and Blood of your Son,
our Lord Jesus Christ.

I pray that this Holy Communion may not bring me condemnation and punishment but forgiveness and salvation.

May it be a helmet of faith and a shield of good will. May it purify me from evil ways and put an end to my evil passions. May it bring me charity and patience, humility and obedience, and growth in the power to do good.

May it be my strong defense against all my enemies, visible and invisible, and the perfect calming of all my evil impulses, bodily and spiritual.

May it unite me more closely to you, the one true God, and lead me safely through death to everlasting happiness with you.

And I pray that you will lead me, a sinner, to the banquet where you, with your Son and Holy Spirit, are true and perfect light, total fulfillment, everlasting joy, gladness without end, and perfect happiness to your saints. Grant this through Christ our Lord. Amen.

– St. Thomas Aquinas

En Ego, O Bone et Dulcissime Iesu

Here, O good and gentle Jesus, I kneel before you, and with all the fervor of my soul I pray that you engrave within my heart lively sentiments of faith, hope, and love, true repentance for my sins, and a firm purpose of amendment. While I see and I ponder your five wounds with great affection and sorrow in my soul, I have before my eyes those words of yours that David prophesied about you: "They have pierced my hands and feet; I can count all my bones" (Psalm 22:17). Amen.

Excerpt from *Lauda Sion Salvatorem*

Come then, Good Shepherd, bread divine,
still show to us thy mercy sign.
O feed us, still keep us thine,
so we may see thy glories shine
in fields of immortality.
O thou, the wisest, mightiest, best,
our present food, our future rest,
come, make us each thy chosen guest,
co-heirs of thine, and comrades blest
with saints whose dwelling is with thee.

– St. Thomas Aquinas

O Sacrum Convivium

O sacred banquet at which Christ is consumed, the memory of His Passion recalled, our soul filled with grace, and our pledge of future glory received!

How delightful, Lord, is Your spirit, which shows Your sweetness to men, offers the precious bread of heaven, fills the hungry with good things, and sends away empty the scornful rich.

V. You have given them bread from heaven.
R. A bread having all sweetness within it.

Let us pray: God, Who left for us a memorial of Your Passion in this miraculous sacrament, grant we implore You, that we may venerate the holy mystery of Your Body and Blood, so that we may ever experience in ourselves the fruitfulness of Your redemption. You who live and reign, world without end. Amen.[40]

– St. Thomas Aquinas

Notes

1. United States Conference of Catholic Bishops, *The Mystery of the Eucharist in the Life of the Church* (Washington, DC: USCCB, 2021), 5, usccb.org (emphasis added).

2. CCC 1324, citing Second Vatican Council, *Lumen Gentium* (November 21, 1964), 11.

3. CCC 1405, citing Ignatius of Antioch, *Letter to the Ephesians* 20.

4. John Paul II, *Dominicae Cenae* (February 24, 1980), 3, vatican.va. The *Catechism* similarly describes the Eucharist as "the memorial of the love with which he loved us 'to the end'" (CCC 1380).

5. Eucharistic Prayer I, *Roman Missal* 89, 90 (and all Eucharistic Prayers). See also Luke 22:14–20.

6. See USCCB, *Mystery of the Eucharist*, 14.

7. Council of Trent (DS 1740), quoted in CCC 1366, referencing 1 Corinthians 11:23, Hebrews 7:24, 27.

8. Council of Trent (DS 1642), quoted in CCC 1376, referencing Matthew 26:26ff, Mark 14:22ff, Luke 22:19ff, 1 Corinthians 24ff.

9. Paul VI, *Mysterium Fidei* (September 3, 1965), 39, quoted in CCC 1374.

10. Congregation for Divine Worship and the Discipline of the Sacraments, *General Instruction of the Roman Missal* (2003), 281, quoted in CCC 1390.

11. Pope Francis @Pontifex, "The Eucharist is essential for us," Twitter, February 28, 2014, 6:28 a.m.

12. Francis, Angelus (June 6, 2021), vatican.va.

13. See Congregations for Divine Worship and the Discipline of the Sacrament, *Redemptionis Sacramentum* (March 25, 2004), 95. See also *Code of Canon Law: New English Translation* (Washington, DC: CLSA, 1998), 921 §2.

14. See CCC 1399, citing Second Vatican Council, *Unitatis Redintegratio* (November 21, 1964), 15.2, and referencing the *Code of Canon Law*, 844 §3.

15. *Unitatis Redintegratio*, 22.3, quoted in CCC 1400.

16. *Unitatis Redintegratio*, 22.3, quoted in CCC 1400.

17. *Unitatis Redintegratio*, 15.2, quoted in CCC 1399, referencing *Code of Canon Law*, 844 §3.

18. See *Code of Canon Law*, 844 §§3–4.

19. *Redemptionis Sacramentum*, 92.

20. *Redemptionis Sacramentum*, 92.

21. USCCB, "The Reception of Holy Communion at Mass," usccb.org.

22. Sacred Congregation for the Discipline of the Sacraments, *Immensae Caritatis*, On Facilitating Reception of Communion in Certain Circumstances (January 29, 1973), 4, available at ewtn.com.

23. *General Instruction of the Roman Missal*, 160.

24. Ignatius of Antioch, Epistle to the Philadelphians 4.

25. See Cale Clarke, "Ancient Evidence for Jesus: Pliny the Younger," *The Faith Explained* (blog), June 4, 2016, thefaithexplained.com.

26. Justin Martyr, *Apology* 1.65–67, quoted in CCC 1345.

27. Hippolytus, *Apostolic Tradition* 1.4, quoted in Everett Ferguson, *The Early Church at Work and Worship*, vol. 3, *Worship, Eucharist, Music, and Gregory of Nyssa* (Eugene, OR: Cascade Books, 2017), 62.

28. USCCB, *Mystery of the Eucharist*, 28.

29. Jorge Mario Bergoglio (Pope Francis), reflection in "The Priesthood and the Holy Eucharist," episode 9 of the EWTN series *La Sagrada Eucaristia*, ewtn.com.

30. Teresa of Calcutta, quoted in USCCB, *Mystery of the Eucharist*, 33.

31. *Code of Canon Law*, 938.3.

32. See CCC 1378 and USCCB, *Compendium Catechism of the Catholic Church*, 286.

33. See CCC 1380 and *Compendium*, 286.

34. Carlo Acutis, quoted in Hannah Brockhaus, "Venerable Carlo Acutis and His Love for the Eucharist," *Catholic News Agency*, June 11, 2020, catholicnewsagency.com.

35. John Paul II, *Dominicae Cenae*, 3, quoted in CCC 1380.

36. Francis, Video Message on the Occasion of the National Eucharistic Congress of India (November 12–15, 2015), vatican.va.

37. Quotation attributed to Mother Teresa, quoted in USCCB, *Mystery of the Eucharist*, 37.

38. John Chrysostom, Homilies on the Gospel of Matthew, 50.3–4, quoted in USCCB, *Mystery of the Eucharist*, 37.

39. Quoted in Philip Kosloski, "Pray This Act of Faith in the Real Presence Before Communion," *Aleteia*, June 1, 2021, aleteia.org. Lightly edited here for style.

40. This translation is by Robert Anderson and Johann Moser, eds., *The Aquinas Prayer Book* (Manchester, NH: Sophia Institute Press, 2000), 61–62.

About the Author

Dr. Edward Sri is a theologian, author, and well-known Catholic speaker who appears regularly on EWTN. Each year he speaks to tens of thousands of people from around the world, including clergy, parish leaders, catechists, and laity.

Dr. Sri has written several best-selling books, including *No Greater Love: A Biblical Walk Through Christ's Passion*, *Walking with Mary*, and *Who Am I to Judge? Responding to Relativism with Logic and Love*. He is also the presenter of several faith formation film series, including *A Biblical Walk Through the Mass*, *Mary: A Biblical Walk with the Blessed Mother*, and *Follow Me: Meeting Jesus in the Gospel of John*, and he is the host of the film series *Symbolon: The Catholic Faith Explained*.

Dr. Sri is a founding leader of FOCUS, the Fellowship of Catholic University Students, where he currently serves as senior vice president of apostolic outreach. He leads pilgrimages to Rome and the Holy Land each year and is the host of the weekly podcast *All Things Catholic*. He holds a doctorate from the Pontifical University of St. Thomas Aquinas in Rome and is an adjunct professor at the Augustine Institute. He lives with his wife, Elizabeth, and their eight children in Littleton, Colorado.